"Nickels Versus Dollars"

Or

How to Turn a Compulsive
Personality Into a Business Asset

National Library of Canada Cataloguing in Publication Data

Hoy, R. Michael
      Nickels or dollars : how to turn a compulsive personality into a business asset /
R. Michael Hoy.
ISBN 1-4120-0800-X
      I. Title.
HF5386.H88 2003   650.1   C2003-903881-5

TRAFFORD

This book was published *on-demand* in cooperation with Trafford Publishing.
On-demand publishing is a unique process and service of making a book available for retail sale to the public taking advantage of on-demand manufacturing and Internet marketing. **On-demand publishing** includes promotions, retail sales, manufacturing, order fulfilment, accounting and collecting royalties on behalf of the author.

Suite 6E, 2333 Government St., Victoria, B.C. V8T 4P4, CANADA

Phone	250-383-6864	Toll-free	1-888-232-4444 (Canada & US)
Fax	250-383-6804	E-mail	sales@trafford.com
Web site	www.trafford.com	TRAFFORD PUBLISHING IS A DIVISION OF TRAFFORD HOLDINGS LTD.	

Trafford Catalogue #03-1168   www.trafford.com/robots/03-1168.html

10   9   8   7   6   5   4   3   2

This book is dedicated to my wife Carol who accompanied me from the very beginning of the journey.

TABLE OF CONTENTS

Chapter 1

The Basics Behind The Personality

4:30 A.M. in the morning and my sleep regimen is complete. I have shifted into first gear for my early routine. For the past several years and probably many years prior to that, I have routinely opened my eyes at this time as if on automatic pilot. Granted, I am a morning person and an early start is not unusual, but this process is so automatic I have no need for an alarm clock. Even if such an early morning requirement as a scheduled airline flight requires that I be at the airport on time, I have enough confidence in this repetitive routine so as to not require a mechanical or electronic device such as an alarm clock.

As to the actual period of sleep, even this is structured on automatic drive. Should I not have a previous engagement, I will turn in at nine o'clock (give or take fifteen minutes). The first three hours will consist of light sleep on and off while listening to public radio, which is an obligatory requirement without which I cannot fall asleep. At about midnight I will go into a deep sleep until my 4:30 A.M. appointment with my morning routine. Does this seem rather overly organized and compulsive? Of course it does, but it is part of the "curse" of the compulsive personality. To a less compulsive person this fixation on organizational detail and systems probably seems absurd and might lead one to comment, and not unjustifiably so, for me to "get a life." Alas, my "curse" continues.

Part and parcel of this personality type seems to require that you be in control of as many aspects of your life as possible. The more systems you have, the more you are in control. I'm not sure how scientific this observation is, however, to this participant, the logic seems to follow.

The process of aging is a journey that is either easier or more difficult depending upon each individual who experiences this inevitable trip, which we must all confront. For me, I don't know which category applies, however my daily exercise routine, which begins immediately upon arising and is followed each and every day without fail, permits me

2

to feel and look good and is part of my "system" of controlling all of those elements in my life of which I am capable. Since as far back as I can remember my weight has always been within five pounds of my current weight and my clothes over the years have not changed in size. I have constructed an exercise routine that covers approximately one hour and a half and it is performed at a leisurely pace each morning, which allows my mind to shift into gear along with my body. My specific routine addresses all parts of my body and keeps me not only feeling good, but maintains flexibility. As you can see from this description, my exercise regimen is another method to control one more aspect of my life. I have made a slight adjustment over the last few years since I have started to "nibble" a bit while watching the television at night. To counter this unnecessary consumption of "junk food" in which I occasionally participate, I have added to my daily exercise routine several exercises at night while I am watching television and after eating those snacks to which many of us are addicted. My justification for indulging myself with these snacks is that (1) the amount consumed is

3

minimal, and (2) the sets of sidebends, situps and leg lifts burn up the added calories. Discipline is a critical part of this regimen and unlike others who consider it a tedious chore to maintain such a routine, the "routine" to me is an integral part of my life. Not only do I anticipate the daily process, but look forward to it as another part of my control mechanism.

The exercise period is over, and my mind and body are in full synchronism. It is time to move on!

Next I head to the bathroom. First order of business, take from the cabinet all of those accoutrements required for this component of the morning routine. Into the medicine cabinet I go and put on the sink top the following: toothbrush, mouthwash, toothpaste, tooth tape (for cleaning between the teeth), shaving cream, shaver, hair brush, comb, deodorant, and shampoo. Once everything is assembled, the routine begins. First I brush my teeth, use tape to clean between the teeth, and finish with mouthwash. Next I lather up and shave, take a nice hot shower, and then finish the routine by brushing, drying, and combing the hair. Pretty neat, huh? This procedure is as predictable as day following night. Dressing to head to work is next, and my clothing and shoes are lined up so a variety of appearances are assured each day.

Before I exit the home, I check my voice mail to ensure no calls came in while I was sleeping and check my computer to ensure that no new e-mails have been sent since I last checked the previous day. As absurd as it may sound, if this routine is not adhered to each morning, the rest of the day will be unstable, just as if a building is constructed and there is a flaw in the base, the structure will be shaky and at risk of tumbling down. Forced analogy maybe, but the reality is in the eye of the beholder.

Chapter 2
The Plot Thickens

Behavior outside of the home and more specifically at the workplace, although similar to that at home, differs in complexity due to the fact that it involves an interface with more people and the structure is quite a bit more complex. For a better perspective on this complexity, it would be instructive to revisit that period when, upon graduation from Boston University, I entered the business world.

By the luck of the draw, my first position out of graduate school was management of a start-up medical testing corporation. I had the fortune of structuring a new company from the start, which gave me the opportunity to use my organizational skills acquired from my experience at graduate school, where I wrote dozens of footnoted papers. It also reinforced my tendency for organization and detail, which had been acquired over the years by cumulative experiences and probably partly from my genetic makeup. Nevertheless, the first two or three years were quite exhilarating and afforded me the opportunity to utilize my theories of organizational structure in an actual business environment. In addition, it allowed me to acquire skills in interacting and managing personnel within the company. During these years the company had a very positive growth and profit curve and my management skills were further enhanced by my newly acquired skill of delegating authority. What a high - to be in a position, right out of graduate school, to sharpen those tools of organization in a real time business situation! Quite a revelation for the novice in this new business atmosphere. In three short years I not only developed my organizational skills, but I began finely tuning my personnel management skill, began to understand the need for profitability and how to get it, and most importantly, I began to tune in to the political nuances present in every business situation.

Oddly enough, all of the above mentioned ingredients to the successful management of a business seemed to fall in place for about the first three years of operation. Not only did my business knowledge base increase exponentially, but also I was financially rewarded in line with my accomplishments.

Beginning of a twenty-year successful business career? Not so fast! As I discussed earlier, control was a central part of this personality profile. Participation in a growing corporation allowed me control in all areas of my involvement except with the board of directors, most of whom were physicians. Here was the beginning of my problem. Physicians by their training generally require that they be in control of their environment. It was easy for them to cede control during the early start up of the corporation, since that which they could control was in the process of "becoming," and therefore control was not a basic issue. I was given leeway to develop the entity from scratch until there was a "critical mass," that is, a profitable and definable entity. At that point my independence began to be compromised. At risk of appearing paranoid, my independent decision-making was being "compromised" by "suggestions" that my performance had not been structured sufficiently, and that if certain controls were implemented, it would facilitate smoother and more efficient growth. In other words, the corporate program was changing and I was being leveraged into complying with this new program. I'm not sure anyone was to blame or that either side was right or wrong. I simply felt a suffocating of my management style and loss of independent decision-making. I guess the analogous situation would be a mother who raises her child, and at age six or seven control of the child is taken out of her hands. As you can well guess, uneasiness was beginning to develop between the board of directors and me. I never had problems dealing with those whom I managed; my problem was with those to whom I had to report at our weekly strategy meetings. The subtle tension was building and it was not only affecting the atmosphere at the office, but was beginning to show at home. This period of subtle and at times not so subtle tension had been building for about six months, so I had a chance to evaluate the advantages and disadvantages of remaining at the corporation. As I have mentioned earlier, "control" was an essential part of my personality and to compromise this critical part of my persona would do nothing but to inject dysfunction into a finely tuned internal system. This being the case, I started to develop a business plan. This plan conflicted with a standing rule that I had developed as part of my conservative approach to employment strategy, and that is "don't leave a job until you find a new position." This fit in with my theory of being in control at all times if possible. What I should have had was a corollary theory of preparing for a new career as soon as you find your current position. In other words, you should assume that your position is temporary and be sure to prepare for your next position. Right or wrong as the theory was, I discussed the situation with my wife and we jointly decided that a change in career would be more productive than continuing in a career that was diminishing in self-fulfillment and to make a move at this time, rather than to permit the situation to evolve into one of a dysfunctional relationship at the office. This in mind, I decided to give my notice the next day. The disclosure to the board was not unexpected, since the directors, most of whom were quite intelligent and circumspect, probably saw the writing on the wall, and were, I suspect, making plans should I leave. Personally, I find this to be one of the most difficult decisions to deal with and I try to put the decision in its proper perspective and assume it is no one's fault. The situation just had evolved wherein the relationship was not working for either side and a mutual disengagement was the only civilized decision that would rectify a deteriorating situation. I have no doubt that some of the directors believed that my decision might be flawed since the corporation seemed to be in a period of growth, which would be good for all parties. What might not have been figured into their equation was my requirement for being "in control." Lest this seem to be an exercise in egotism, such is not the case. Some people need to be in control of their lives, which includes control of their jobs. For these poor souls, there is no option but to take charge of the situation or fall into line and subject themselves to a lifetime of frustrations functioning in situations where they have no opportunity to exercise the control that their personality requires. As you will see later, this is certainly not a black and white analysis and this word "control" can have a not so clear definition.

Wow! What do we have here? As you can see, when I am in "my" world, I have complete control, or as much as humanly possible with minimal outside influence. Now I have encountered my first barrier - conflict between my goals and those of the outside institution with which I am involved. The winner? Neither side, may I suggest. The corporation lost one valuable asset. It was obvious, at least to this observer, that my input into the growth of the corporation was very positive. How does one put a value on a manager who has brought the corporation from zero to a very profitable growth position? I am sure that another manager might have duplicated my creative and positive contribution, but what I did was a fact and what might have happened without my input is speculation. Whichever side you may come down upon, excellent management is hard to find regardless of the potential pool of talent in the workforce. On the other hand, I might have bitten off my nose to spite my face in that I lost the leverage that one acquires through corporate involvement.

Instead of using the corporate leverage to accelerate my growth in business, I was now on my own and had to create an entity from scratch. A short-term tactical error, perhaps, but my position was that there was a sacrifice involved to maintain the "control" required given my personality type. To choose otherwise might have compromised the larger picture, thus frustrating my long-term goals. Nevertheless, the decision was made and on I must continue with the journey.

Chapter 3
Time To Go It Alone

Enter what we shall call my "blue" period, so called because I associate the color blue with a cool, moody, and somewhat melancholy feeling. After having worked in a system where I had a personal secretary and a team of coworkers to assist me with executing my game plan, being self-employed, (and yes, that was the decision I made so I could be in full control of my actions,) was quite a shock to the system. Although intellectually I understood what to expect without a support system, psychologically it revealed the complexity of "going it alone."

I had accumulated reserve cash for just such a situation, so cash flow would not be an issue for six to nine months. During this period of time I shall always be most grateful to my wife who was working, which took some of the bite off this shock to the system and her psychological support was critical if I was to be successful in this new venture. No matter how much one tries to prepare for such a change in direction, the next morning upon completion of your structured routine, you are faced with the absence of routine for the remainder of the day.

As we shall see, the *theory* of starting your own business and the *reality* of a creative venture are two different animals. The first obstacle I encountered, and it is much easier to quantify in hindsight, was my definition of exactly what type of business I would be proposing for myself. I knew that my strength was organization, but it took a while for me to add two important ingredients: (l) financial management and (2) real estate. It seems so simple in retrospect, but at the time I had only worked in a sheltered environment, the corporation, and there is a vast difference between managing a defined entity and actually making up a new organization.

This taught me an important truth, namely, it is one thing to manage and make grow an existing entity, and quite another process to "create" a new entity. There are two separate skills involved. One is the ability to organize and manage, and the other is a creative process of making something out of nothing.

15

There are some people, not many I believe, who have both skills - the entrepreneurial ability to make something out of nothing and the managerial types who can structure and manage anything that is thrown their way. My particular skill happens to be the managerial talent, which comes naturally, I believe. It is harder for me to execute that other part of the equation, that is, the ability to initiate a new entity. Talent in either area is not a matter of intelligence or lack thereof; rather it is the fact that some people are just better in one of the two disciplines.

Figuring out this fact took me about two years of trial and error. I took on quite a few "accounts" in this process of self-discovery. The accounts I dabbled in during this period ranged from accounting services for individuals and small companies, financial planning for individuals, managing small real estate corporations, and several other small ventures too insignificant to mention. This was my "blue" period, and although I earned a fairly good living and was able to purchase a home and invest in the stock market, I had not established what I could reasonably define as my career.

Having this compulsive personality does have some advantages. Having put myself out on a limb, I was forced to make decisions. Making decisions has never been a problem, since being so structured by definition requires one to be constantly organizing and reorganizing. The fact that I had a game plan simply meant I would have to take it from the drawing board to the finished product. Getting from point A to point B was easier said than done. Since I knew the direction and goal, what would be simpler than following my own directions to the finished product? The dilemma which presented itself was that implementing a game plan doesn't always follow in a straight line.

The first impediment to my goal was that the accounts I had targeted as the foundation for my newly formed business were not precisely as I had envisioned them. Quite a few of these target accounts ended up being dead-end situations which were not what I had envisioned as building blocks for the new consulting company. The quandary in which

I found myself was that a period of time was involved to evaluate the accounts before discarding them. The accounts might be too small, with no growth potential, or would not give me the autonomy needed to build them to conform to my system. Again, why gather various accounts that would not permit me to configure them into a structure upon which I could build? Yet again, I was at that juncture where if I made the wrong decision I would be back where I was two years earlier.

An illustration of the complexity and time involved in this decision-making might be in order to demonstrate the problem. An account that I acquired by simply responding to an advertisement in the local paper seemed promising. The advertisement required a consultant to manage a real estate office in the Boston area. This seemed tempting at first observation, but as we shall see, first impressions may be deceiving.

Chapter 4

This Is A Little More Complex Than I Envisioned

The process of meeting a new client is an interesting event. From my point of view, I know he is in need of a service. On one level, it is my object to convince him that my service is that for which he has advertised. This includes being a good listener to hear what he is really saying, while at the same time structuring my answers to fit his needs. A cat and mouse game? Maybe. On another level, it is incumbent upon me to evaluate what he is saying, while at the same time convince myself that this is the account that will fit my business strategy. Years earlier it was most important that I make a good impression to capture an account or position. Today, although this is still true, it is ever so more important that I approve of the potential client. Part of this revision of priorities is age and experience, but a more significant issue is that control factor which keeps appearing over and over again. I have found that it is not as important to generate new accounts as it is to have the accounts fit my management requirements, namely, accounts that I really manage.

As regards this particular account, I was eased into a position that seemed to cede to me the autonomy that I required to effectively manage and build the account. As the program advanced, I found that I had my system of management, and the owner had his, which he decided to retain. When the management systems did not cross, my autonomy was kept intact, however in those areas where his and my authority overlapped, I would, of course, come in second. The reader might observe that since it is his company, he should have the final say. This would be true if he were a better manager than I, however, the reason he hired me was that he was in need of management, or at least I thought this was the case.

One of the dilemmas that I could never quite resolve was the eventuality that could occur when the manager and owner would come head to head on an issue. In most cases, the potential conflict is resolved, or at least managed, when one side or the other backs down. I have always been able to bite my tongue, swallow a bit of pride, and move on, however on those occasions when this was not possible, I always had the ultimate option of resigning. My defense for such situations, short of resigning, was to go into my shell of organization. What would in effect evolve were two management systems. I would establish a geographic location in the company and set up my system for which I had responsibility. For example, if the owner was disorganized and sloppy, that was his problem. In my designated area, all systems would be neatly organized where I made use of an often-used phrase that "for everything there is a place, and there is a place for everything."

This approach for defining and organizing my territory within the company accomplished the following: (1) my comfort level was reinforced since my territory was neatly organized and functional, (2) my responsibilities were well-defined with a paperwork backup system, and (3) this strategy allowed me to be responsible for only those areas within my jurisdiction. It would become a good defense mechanism if something went awry elsewhere in the organization and it could not lead to my department. As paranoid as this may appear, and I am sure that there are many readers who share my feelings and have had similar experiences, it reinforced my need for backup in a company atmosphere in which I had minimal confidence in areas other than those for which I had responsibility.

This not being a perfect world, my strategy worked in an overwhelming percentage of the situations with which I was faced. However, there were always a small number of instances when what I might call "company problems" arose, and if these included my department, I had to respond. So although my "sub-system" management strategy worked when I could isolate the problem and solve it through my own means, these "company problems" required that I participate in a company solution, which allowed me minimal flexibility in solving the problem. The resulting solution, in my view, was less than excellent.

I am sure that you will conclude from this exposition that it would be next to impossible for me to function in a system in which I did not control to my satisfaction. I will have to agree, with the caveat that this is an imperfect world and absolutes such as "complete control" do not exist. Part of the burden that I must carry during my journey is to practically define at which point in a given situation I must cede some of my control for the good of not sacrificing more.

This particular work situation resolved itself amicably between the owner and me. I will say in my defense that I have always had a positive ongoing relationship with most of the owners with whom I have associated.

At the end of this relationship, I sat down with the owner and we discussed why it was not possible for us to continue the relationship. My confession to him was that (1) the lack of efficiency and neatness was more than I could abide, and (2) when I was first hired, I expected to be involved in top management decisions. As it turned out, he wanted to make all of the decisions and my role was simply to implement those decisions.

His evaluation of me was that although he had no reservations regarding my efficiency and talent, I put too much pressure on him in terms of schedules and he found it impossible to conform to my management requests, which put him under unnecessary stress.

We discussed these subjects over a meal and when we parted we remained friends, and I still consider him a friend today.

As you can see from the previous example, this process of establishing a new account is both exhaustive and time consuming. As tedious a process as it is, each new account was both an adventure and a learning experience. As similar as each account was, each had its own unique complexion from the structure of the company to the individual personality of the owner and each employee. The process was also a contradiction for me in that establishing new accounts was a growing experience, thus adding to my portfolio of knowledge. But at the same time, it exposed me to "change" which I didn't welcome at the time and I still resist to this day. You see, to the compulsive personality, at least to this obsessively compulsive personality, change is threatening to my system of stability and predictability. Maintaining a system is my safety blanket and allows me to control that which I know and that with which I feel comfortable. I know intellectually that change is as inevitable as day following night and I accept it reluctantly! Nevertheless, I continue my journey.

Having this "condition" is not necessarily a handicap, unless, like anything else in life, one carries it to the extreme. In our personal life, my wife and I bought a home upon my graduation from graduate school at Boston University. My logical and obsessive tendency dictated that buying a home as soon as possible was a good financial decision. Since as far back as we can trace the history of real estate in this country, purchase of a primary residence has been a good investment over the long term. This being the case, we gathered all of the capital we had on hand, which was very little at the time, and acquired our first major asset, although highly leveraged with a mortgage. It is interesting that we never thought that we could afford that first home, but somehow we generated the income necessary to maintain this newly acquired asset.

Chapter 5

A Little History Is In Order

In one's lifetime, luck is also a factor, but as I always tell my wife, "the harder you work, the luckier you get." We bought this first home in 1973 when we stretched to accumulate a down payment on a $35,000 starter home. As luck would have it, within six years, which is how long we held our first home, the market value of the homes in this area of the country almost tripled! Part of this good timing, of course, was luck. We bought our home at the beginning of a real estate boom. Yes, we were lucky, but if we hadn't committed to buying a home at that time, we would not have had this unexpected nest egg. As it turned out, we sold the home, paid off the mortgage, and had a substantial down payment to invest in our "dream home" south of Boston.

During our six-year stay in our first home, we also set up a 401K savings plan when the program first began, and again, as luck would have it, we built our deferred savings plan substantially over the years.

Being very conservative, we diversified our portfolio on the conservative side so that even to this day with the ups and downs of the market, we have shown growth over the years with some years more profitable than others.

In the life cycle there is a beginning, middle, and end, and for this person this means that there is no space for procrastination. Life consists of a series of challenges and these challenges represent potential roadblocks which, when encountered, must be overcome. Our "dream home" south of Boston by the ocean represented one such challenge. Not only was acquiring this valuable asset a challenge, but taking what was an unfinished new home, and through what might be called a superhuman effort, we finished and transformed it into one of our prime assets.

Referring back to the luck factor, granted there was a real estate boom, but the mortgage interest rates were above 16%, and to purchase a home in this milieu was indeed a challenge. Looking back, the decision was easy because with hindsight how could one not invest in real estate during a real estate boom? From the perspective of the early 1980s however, with that high mortgage interest rate, even though we had strong feelings that the rate could not sustain such a high level, making the commitment to purchase at that time was indeed a challenge. Only those in similar circumstances can appreciate the effort for two people, while both working full time, to invest the time and energy to not only finish the home, but also to make changes to meet our specifications, furnish the home, and landscape an acre of land. Fortunately, my wife's personality is almost as compulsive as mine, and between us we ensured that with this major project there was indeed a beginning, middle, and end. Some might question the end portion of the process, though, since changes are always presenting themselves, thus making the ending portion of the equation more gray than black.

After a full five years of participating in this interesting undertaking, we had, at least for the most part, accomplished our goal of maximizing the value of the asset. I must admit however, that the five years were not all pain. The process of building this asset was mostly enjoyable to both of us, and although many a night we would be exhausted, it was an enjoyable exhaustion and gave us many hours of discussing how we could improve what was already a valuable asset.

An observation might be in order for those so disposed to purchasing and improving upon such a real estate asset. Maintenance is an ingredient that is relevant not only to real estate, but to all aspects of life. Without it, no asset will retain or gain in value. Maintenance in any aspect of your life demands a discipline in your activities throughout your life. I have always found that good habits are as easy to acquire as bad habits. The maintenance of the home consisted of ongoing chores which simply kept the house in tiptop shape and included lawn maintenance, replacing plants when required, and keeping the street in front of the house always looking good for that "curb appeal" should we decide to sell the asset. In addition, there were major maintenance projects, like having the house painted every five years, replacing the roof (a hopefully once in a lifetime project,) and periodic upgrading of our clay tennis court which is required about every three or four years. As you can see, maintenance is an integral part of keeping the property in the kind of shape that will guarantee, as much as humanly possible, the best return on our investment should we decide to sell. I believe the same theory applies here that, as mentioned earlier, applies to your job, that is, being prepared to sell the home while living there even if you don't plan to sell. The discipline required in this process fed right into our basic personalities, and instead of the process being one of drudgery, it was a positive part of our life that we thoroughly enjoyed.

Our program for upkeep of the property led to another area that required ongoing care, namely record keeping and budgeting. Over the years, we had always been good record keepers. Keeping with our philosophy that "for everything there is a place and there is a place for everything," all incoming bills were put into an open folder, and all paid bills with our computerized bill stubs went into the closed file. At the end of the year, the records for the entire year were put into a box and filed in the basement, so each year we began with a new batch of bills, and bills from previous years were in boxes labeled by year. We now added a budgeting program to this system of record keeping.

Since all of our records are in the computer, it was easy enough to generate a yearly budget. Most people have no idea, if you ask them, how much it costs them to live each year in terms of cash. Our computerized budget system allowed us not only to document our current yearly expenses, but we could compare it to previous years and then project what our expenses would be for the upcoming year. Once we disciplined ourselves to conform to this budget format, and as you can guess, given our compulsiveness, this was no problem, implementing and maintaining it was a cinch. Comparing our joint income to our projected expenses allowed us to project how much we could save each year, how much to allow for vacations, and how to finance any new projects we might consider. If more people took this approach to their finances, their lives, I believe, would be much simpler and the level of stress would be reduced considerably. As mentioned earlier, good habits are as easy to develop as are bad habits.

Perhaps the question comes down to how precise and organized you deem necessary. Those of us who might fall into this "extreme" category might be overly organized if observed by a "normal" person. For example, here are some illustrations of this attention to detail that might confirm this excessive behavior.

When I cash a check, I will take the bills given me by the teller at the bank and before putting the bills into my wallet, I will ensure that all the bills are facing in the same direction and also ensure that no bill has a corner folded. This is really extreme!

I carry with me each day an appointment book. At the beginning of each year, I mark for a full year in advance all of those processes or appointments that are done on either a regular or repetitive basis during the year and these are marked on the appropriate dates for the entire year. This will ensure that no ongoing procedure is missed during the year. These are items such as car inspections, quarterly estimated taxes, birthdays, and so on. As regards daily "to do" items, they are marked on the current page of the appointment book, and when completed are erased daily, so I end each day with a blank calendar page. Although this might seem rather bizarre, you must admit, it is efficient.

In a notebook, I itemize my monthly expenses broken down weekly. This is done for each month in advance so as to allow me to budget for the month and ensure that all bills are paid on time. If by some chance a bill does not come in the mail, it alerts me that a given bill has not been sent and that I should call the source to ensure that my credit rating is not adversely affected due to an error on the part of the company to whom I owe a balance.

The above samples are just an indication as to how both my wife and I structure our journey through the complexities of life. Observers might posit the thought that this structure is too intense and time consuming, however, if you program yourself to incorporate all of these details into your routine, the process becomes part of your life. Far from being cumbersome, it in fact makes your life simpler and the process becomes almost invisible and an integral part of your life.

Chapter 6

So You Want To Have A Consulting Business

My consulting business had been honed down to several stable accounts which, at this point, had given me: (1) the autonomy in each account so I could maintain that control necessary to fit my management style, (2) economic security by generating enough income to satisfy my definition of where I thought I should be positioned financially at this point, and (3) one or more of the current accounts might evolve to a place that would afford me full management of a growing entity, allowing me to display those management skills to creatively structure and manage a venture that might expand into any number of directions.

This type of creative atmosphere required an owner with vision and the capacity to see in me the potential to manage a company for him. In other words, I needed an "advocate" who could envision unlimited expansion in any number of directions, with the confidence to delegate to me the authority that I required to creatively grow his company. I, in turn, would delegate authority under my management while at the same time setting up a complex set of controls to ensure that accountability and responsibility were present at all levels, including mine.

One of the potential pitfalls of my theory was that I assumed that one or more of the owners of these companies that I had identified as possible stepping stones to a larger and more expansive program might not have the ability or mindset to identify in me the potential to do much more than that for which he contracted. If, for example, a particular owner hired me to solve accounting problems, once the problem had been solved, did he visualize me as a convenient vehicle for solution of that problem and stop there since I had solved his current problem? Or, did he go to another level and say to himself that I had accounting talent, but maybe, since I very adequately fulfilled his needs in this area, maybe I had additional talents that could help him further grow his company? Herein lies the problem in many cases. For whatever reasons, an owner might only want that specific problem solved and doesn't need help in expanding his company in a more general sense, or he doesn't see the potential in this consultant to expand his services, or, heaven forbid, he doesn't see in this consultant the ability to expand in areas other than accounting.

I must add at this point some self-criticism. Having reached at this point a comfort level, I became somewhat complacent. I had so organized the accounts that maintaining them became a rote exercise. My attention became focused in other areas, such as buying land in Florida and building a home on that land, which was in a closed community on a golf course.

My whole life was running so smoothly and I had so much free time that my wife and I devoted much of it to golf and developing our second home in Florida. I was also developing a financial portfolio and projecting the time when we would reach "critical mass" financially and be able to live on unearned income. These goals and projects, all noble and worthwhile, lulled me into not focusing on my career in business. As is usually the case, when you don't focus on goals, they become vague and indistinct. There was a period of maybe three years during which I floated in this state of limbo without feeling pain, since I had structured my life so as not to expose myself to any financial hardships.

Chapter 7

Into Each Life A Little Rain Must Fall

One morning as I entered the office of one of my major accounts, I was informed that the owner had suddenly passed away the night before. This was a totally unexpected occurrence, however, in retrospect, I should have been preparing for this eventuality since the owner was in her upper seventies and it was questionable as to how much longer she would be capable of managing this company. Her becoming incapacitated might have been in the back of my mind, but her death was totally shocking to my system. Again, because of my lack of attention to this detail due to my pursuit of collateral goals, this event presented itself to me in a most unexpected manner. As it turns out, this was to be a seminal event in my business career, as I will later divulge.

The account itself did not have the potential for developing into a larger and more complex management opportunity and my responsibilities were mostly accounting activities. Again, I was lulled into a sense of false security since the remuneration was quite adequate for the minimal time and energy spent on the account.

The owner, an elderly self-made millionaire, had many real estate holdings with quite a positive cash flow. I conjecture that, on one level, since the account was quite substantial in size, and with her advancing age, I assumed that I would be the logical manager of all aspects of her business since I was in such a critical position of managing the cash flow. This would turn out to be a serious misjudgment on my behalf as would presently be revealed to me.

Since she was a self-made millionaire with minimal education, she did not have a sophisticated approach to running the business. My arrival on the scene was only prompted by the fact that she was in the middle of an IRS investigation that revealed shoddy accounting procedures, and resulted in a fine and warning that her books would have to be updated and maintained on a professional basis. Thus my entrance into the company.

Upon inspection of her records, I found that there was no system, and business procedures were addressed on a day-to-day basis with virtually no organized system of record keeping. Viewing this situation, I believed that I had an unbelievable opportunity to create from this chaos a system that would be "my" system. I could construct a business plan that would take those disparate elements that currently existed and formulate a strong business plan. An organized system with both accountability and form would result. I could demonstrate to the owner that from the chaotic situation that currently existed, we could structure a business plan that would (a) relieve her of the day-to-day tedium which she was not performing, and (b) allow me the opportunity to demonstrate to her the advantage of having a manager. I would not only structure and implement a business plan, but also present to her on a regular basis a view of the company as it grew. This would give her the feeling that the weight of managing the company was not entirely on her shoulders and free her to see the big picture with a less obstructed view.

What a prime opportunity for both parties, or at least so I thought. Of course this was a great opportunity for me, but wasn't this also a great opportunity for her to relieve herself of the tedium of day-to-day details and permit her the view from the top? This in mind, I began what I thought to be a journey to realize the dreams of both parties.

From the ever so perfect perspective of hindsight, this was an account that turned out to be a trap. It was part of a design which, and I must concede a mistake on my part, kept me from making a decision regarding the efficacy of this account becoming a catalyst for developing into a prime management account.

From the outset, I was given almost complete control of the accounting system. No interference was forthcoming from the owner due to the fact that (1) the history with the IRS involvement left the owner with a fear that, if her financial house was not put in order, a revisit by that feared organization might ensue, (2) her knowledge of professional accounting procedures was minimal, and (3) as I developed my accounting system, she saw that it functioned almost flawlessly, at least as far as she could see. A trust developed between us, at least as regards her financial record keeping.

On the downside of this interesting relationship was the fact that as I attacked this uncontrolled system, a gargantuan effort was undertaken to establish, almost from ground level, righting of this floundering giant. In the process I became so busy in the next year that I did not recognize the larger picture of establishing an overall management system.

The first clue that a full management system would not eventuate occurred to me when my attempts at computerizing this monster account were rebuffed by the owner on several occasions. Not that there were confrontations, but she had her ways of delaying and procrastinating, which she had craftily developed over the years, and I must admit were quite effective.

In terms of my compulsive personality, organizing this untamed monster was indeed challenging and fully tested all of my organizational skills.

This was an exhilarating trip through which I could demonstrate to the owner how I could "take charge" of this chaotic situation. There was latitude in decision-making due to the fact that, while I worked three mornings a week at the office, she came in only in the afternoons to manage her beauty salon, which was located next door. Our paths seldom crossed, except when I would be in need of her signature on checks payable to suppliers or taxes. To this day I do not understand why she spent so much time at her beauty salon, which generated minimal income, while right next door in my office hundreds of thousands of dollars were flowing through the office. I can only conclude that since the beauty salon was her first business years earlier, she felt, however illogically, that this was her main business. Maybe addressing the massive paperwork involved in maintaining the real estate part of the business might overwhelm her.

This state of affairs on a tactical level was quite advantageous for me since it permitted me virtual autonomy to structure the financial format for the company. However, as regards the larger picture, my future in bona fide management of this account, it turned out to be a blind spot for me. The fact that I did not see her on a daily basis let me avoid the consequence of confronting her with questions of my management position in the company. Be that as it may, the result was a period of procrastination that broke one of my major rules of self-discipline. I was so busy building an accounting system that I pushed the management question into the background and lost focus on my main objective.

Looking back, she did not have the capacity to delegate authority, whether it was because she trusted no one in business except herself or whether she had the same element in her personality that I have, the need to be in control.

Of course the whole issue became academic upon her death when, before I knew it, the large family, along with a bevy of attorneys, came in like vultures for a kill. There were quite a few properties involved in the estate worth several millions of dollars. This kind of estate will generate quite a bit of attention, believe me! Before I knew it, all control of the business was put into the hands of the attorneys. Between the family members and the attorneys, I was relieved of any control I might have had, and thus ended my consulting services for the account.

Chapter 8

The Rain Stops, Enter Some Blue Sky

As odd as it may seem, termination of this account brought my long-term strategy back into focus. Interestingly, my very compulsiveness hindered my vision of the big picture and my main focus by diverting my attention for an entire year or so on the multitude of details involved in managing the accounting aspects of the various pieces of real estate.

Put yourself in the shoes of the obsessively organized person who is confronted with the myriad of interrelated problems. You can, I presume, sympathize with my fixation on organizing the accounts and setting up a system to take what was a massive amount of paperwork, separate it into its constituent parts, and build a system for each piece of real estate.

Theory and reality at times intersect, and at that juncture, under certain circumstances we have the option of applying our theory of a given situation to the reality at hand. In other cases, the reality of a situation can be so overwhelming that response is on a practical basis and only later do we have the luxury of applying the theoretical construct to the current situation. Such I believe was the case under discussion. In my defense, the period of time about which we are discussing was quite busy and intense. Granted, part of my philosophy of work was that one should be looking for another account even as one is under contract with one's current owner. It was so hectic during this period of time, my full concentration was not dedicated to the current account. Only after the fact did I realize that (1) I should have been pursuing a new account should one of my present accounts disappear, and (2) I should have recognized, given the personality makeup of the owner, that this account would not be leading to a comprehensive management of her company.

The disappearance of this account from my portfolio left a void both in terms of time and thinking space. Fortunately I had accumulated a fairly good cash reserve over the years and my current cash flow could easily cover current expenses. Also, we had two homes without mortgages and carried literally no open bills. Still, no one turns down extra income so losing the income from the account, which was one of my major sources of income, was bothersome. On the other hand, I was left with the freedom of time to more objectively examine that larger picture to which I occasionally refer.

I always discuss decision-making with my wife, and on more than one occasion we discuss "nickel versus dollar" decisions. In more specific terms, the fact that there are everyday decisions one makes that don't effect the "big picture," but there are those occasional forks in the road when one must make the right decision, for this decision may or in all probability will contribute to a major directional change in your life. This was one of those decision-making times!

What a blessing it was to be able to sit back without the stress of my usual heavy workload. Part of my personality profile seems to be that almost every moment of the day must be filled with one activity or the other. This was a new experience and I must admit, quite pleasurable. This was a time for soul searching and would not only allow me to sum up where I have been, but to analyze where I currently stood and project where I chose to be in the future.

Firstly, the stress, real or imaginary, of financial security had always been foremost in my thinking. I suspect it was part of the baggage I had assumed because of my less than affluent childhood. I had always viewed those circumstances surrounding me as I grew up, and they all seemed to be at least a rung or more above me. This can be a dangerous perspective since excessive materialism or any other excess might color decision-making as you travel through life. Be that as it may, this was my perspective, developed in my formative years and I hope I have since been able to position it in a clearer luminosity. The brighter side of this perspective is that it has permitted me to reach a point where I have essentially attained that position of having reached "critical mass" economically, which allows me to exist on unearned income and "work" becomes an option rather than a necessity. The fact that I have successfully met the challenges of economic survival must not be an end in and of itself. It simply means that I can now pursue other non-economic goals and let blossom that portion of my persona which until now has been repressed, for lack of a better word, by my focus on things material. With this newly acquired freedom, an analysis of my current accounts was needed to determine if changes were in order to restructure my future.

Chapter 9

Time For An Introspective Look At The Consulting Business

Upon inspection of my portfolio of accounts, there were several small accounts that I decided to leave intact. These accounts were inconsequential in terms of income, and could be managed at home on my computer, as they consumed minimal time to maintain. There were two other accounts that required some analysis to see if adjustments were in order.

The first of these main accounts was an account that I have maintained for almost twenty years, and the owner, a physician, has become a personal friend. This account, although not a big income earner, has been steady over the years and, unlike the above-mentioned account, allowed me almost total autonomy. Perhaps this is one of the reasons why it has run so smoothly over the years.

A short summary might be in order to clarify the history of the account. Back in the early 1980s I met this physician through my wife, who at the time worked in the business office at a hospital in the Boston area where the physician was also employed. Since it has been such a long time, I forget specifically how we came to forge this relationship; however, it came to my attention that she was interested in acquiring some real estate and upon acquisition, the property would require management.

I had just started my management company and this appeared to be an interesting potential account. At any rate, I happened to locate an apartment building that was for sale, and after various negotiations I acquired the property on behalf of the physician and thus began our relationship. Not only was this my first account established under the new management company, but also it was a testing ground for my management skills.

What an extraordinary opportunity for me to display my management skills and establish this account as the anchor for my newly developing management company. It also helped me to define specifically what I was taking on for my first major account. They say that those situations that are symbiotic, that is, good for both parties, are those that have optimal chance for success. This, I believe, was one of those situations. Here was a physician who was in need of an investment property with management built in, and I happened to be a business manager who was looking for that first major account with which to jump-start my new business.

My energy at this time was quite intense in that not only did I want to impress the new owner, but also this would be the first company for which I would be constructing from the ground an entire business plan. For the first time since I left the medical testing corporation, it was my responsibility to "create" the operational system for this new company. The significant difference was that I had no staff on site. I had resources, but those were for services required and for which I would pay on an "as needed" basis. I'm not sure if I was just lucky or an excellent manager, but for the period this property was owned, operational problems were minimal and a good bottom line profit was generated for the owner. My management fee was determined by how efficiently I ran the company. My compulsive personality was challenged in maintaining a smoothly flowing company. With my ability to manage effectively, I found that tenant complaints and maintenance in general were under control. I used a rule that I maintain to this day, which is if you pay your suppliers (electricians, plumbers, repairmen, and so on) on a timely basis (within a week to ten days) they will show up regularly, the problem will be solved, and tenant relations in general will be excellent. This policy, which helped immeasurably in tenant relations, allowed the tenants to feel that if you cared this much for the building by responding to their needs and the building was generally kept in good repair, then it was "their" building and they would treat it accordingly. Of course, no business relationship exists without disagreements and this relationship is no exception. The owner and I have had discussions over the years of maximizing profitability versus operational efficiency. On the one hand she believes that the properties should generate top rents, especially during "boom" times in the economy. Although I don't disagree with the philosophy, the "devil is in the detail," as is the case with all things in life. From an operational point of view, I don't think you should ever under rent, except in case of emergency. On the other hand, the difference between a good and reasonable rent and top rent, I think has to be determined by (1) the nature of the tenant, such as an excellent payer who helps keep the property in top shape, or the marginal tenant who doesn't help increase the value of the property, and (2) if you go for the highest possible rent, you may be cutting off your nose to spite your face because of possible vacancies until you can get that top rental of the apartment. There is a delicate balance between getting the highest possible rent for a unit and minimizing possible management and cash flow problems, which could result in unexpected problems that increase your management costs in terms of time and efficient dealing with dissatisfied tenants and tenant turnover. This is an ongoing debate we have had, and I believe each respects the other's arguments. For my part, I try to get the maximum rents for the owner while at the same time minimizing management expenses and tenant problems. Management is a creative process, and demands flexibility.

My remuneration for management of the building was quite adequate and was directly related to the fact that I delegated responsibility to many of my suppliers, with appropriate control mechanisms. This minimized the time required by me to solve on-site problems. The rule of delegation of authority has stayed with me through the years and has taught me that if you have confidence in your management style, delegation of authority, far from decreasing your management position, increases your ability to accomplish much more in terms of overall management, and, with the proper controls, allows you a better view of the "big picture" since you are not mired down in the minutia of the system.

On a philosophic level, I maintain that one needs an "advocate" who can recognize talent and is circumspect and confident enough to see in that person the potential for growth, and is in a position to reinforce that growth. This particular owner was such an advocate, but unfortunately the account never grew to the size where my full potential could be realized in a larger venue, such as several buildings with unrestricted growth.

I must however, at this point, take responsibility for not feeding into this advocacy by encouraging the owner to purchase additional buildings using this building for leverage. I refer to remarks made earlier that some people are excellent managers who can take existing entities and efficiently manage them, and others have that entrepreneurial bent which permits them to commit to new unstructured ventures. Part of my obsessive compulsiveness, as I have mentioned earlier, is that I perform best where there is a beginning, middle, and end, and I seem to function optimally in taking existing entities and efficiently managing them.

This said, I did locate this property for the owner, which certainly took an entrepreneurial touch. But alas, at a time when I should have encouraged the owner to leverage the building and possibly locate additional investors to commit to a larger project, my organized, maybe overly organized, mind "shut down" to this option. The end result of this missed opportunity was that the apartment building was sold, and a smaller property was purchased which I manage to this day. An opportunity lost? Perhaps, but at this particular juncture, my requirement to be "in control" and stubbornness, for lack of a better word, precluded my decision to create new ground.

This was one of those critical junctures in life where my decision at that time, in part determined my current position. Although I am economically comfortable today, whether making another less conservative decision at that time would have opened new and challenging conditions shall remain academic.

The final account that requires definition so as to decide the appropriate resolution is an account that I have had as part of my portfolio. It is an unusual account in that, although it has some of the characteristics of that account mentioned earlier where the owner passed away, there are significant differences. Again, it was a family-owned business, and I will not stop here to discuss the nature of family-owned businesses compared to professionally managed businesses, other than to mention that this was sort of a "classic" example of the difference between the two.

The opportunity at the outset seemed to be tailor-made for my management capabilities, and again I had that energy surge in tackling such a potentially challenging account.

The ingredients seemed present for an interesting relationship. First, there were various properties that the family owned, and management certainly was required. Secondly, the key and only owner involved was an attorney who was just beginning his practice. Thirdly, as a base we had an office building which would make an ideal location from which we could operate the company. Fourthly, my assumption was that the attorney would run his practice out of the office building as a separate entity and I would manage the real estate portion of the family business. We could have monthly meetings when I could update him on the operation for the month. In my eyes, a perfect format for a relationship where I could act as the vehicle for expansion of the family business.

There are curious turns in life, and one must expect the unexpected. As was the case with the owner who passed away, this owner was a "control freak" and I don't use the word in a demeaning or disparaging sense since I also tend to have those characteristics. Whether or not he was defensive about giving out authority due to insecurity or he just plain had a requirement that he be in control of everything, the end result was that he wanted to manage both his law firm and the real estate operation. As I mentioned earlier, some people can be both a management wizard and a successful entrepreneur at the same time. This was not the case here because neither operation was being managed properly and the results were palpable in the physical appearance of the building and the cluttered paperwork system at the office. I have no doubt that I was a more capable manager because of my background. We had two different mindsets. I took on projects and expeditiously completed them, while he was the opposite and a procrastinator. He either finished projects at the last minute or responded when the issue became a crisis. My obligation in the relationship was to perform in the role of accountant and ensure that bills and taxes got paid. This was a shock to my system in that I could certainly perform accounting activities to ensure bills were paid on time and taxes kept current. This, however, was not how I envisioned my role in the company, but since I was being paid a very adequate compensation, between this and my other accounts, life was financially very satisfying.

During this period of time, which was over two years, I was chomping at the bit, because I saw operational shortcomings that were not being addressed and ran counter to my philosophy regarding tenant relations and building maintenance. Again, during this time I saw parts of my autonomy, which I require, subtly downsized and I found myself making decisions at a much lower level than that to which I was accustomed. The owner was always quite polite and we had a civilized relationship. However, when you are making decisions at a much lower level than that which you have experienced, you become uneasy. This level of uneasiness began to reflect itself in my attitude. I found that I would arrive at the office and instead of being inspired and motivated, I began counting the hours before I could leave. This was not a positive condition and again, my healthy cash flow permitted me to stagnate in this state of affairs longer than should have been the case. Not that I was oblivious to the situation, because at another level I was analyzing how close I was to "critical mass" economically so that should I have to make a decision, I was prepared.

It was about this time that the owner to whom I previously referred passed away, and with the diminution of her account, the financial situation became less attractive and I began seriously thinking about restructuring my life. About a year prior to this confluence of events, I began writing a novel. I had been mulling this creative venture around in my head on and off for several years. I had envisioned a career as a writer, but due to the economics that I mentioned earlier, I had decided upon the more practical career in business.

My meeting with the owner was probably an appointment that we had mutually been expecting. It was difficult for me to conceal my feelings, and he had probably been bothered by my attempts, as subtle as they were, to push my decision-making beyond the accounting parameters. Since we were both intelligent individuals, it was inevitable that this mutual feeling of uneasiness surface and be resolved and not left to fester.

Our meeting was incidental, as most of our meetings were. I'm not sure if he felt unease in scheduling formal meetings, since when they occurred our meetings ran along parallel lines and never really met. From my point of view, I believe that he felt he had to be in control of the meetings and dictate the agenda. These infrequent meetings led to frustration on my part since I found it difficult, if not impossible, to develop my theme. My attempts became atrophied since I could not keep his attention on the subject at hand or he declined participation in my agenda. It was the little things that became most frustrating for me. For example, when he had a project that he wished me to implement, he would not only explain the project to me, but would then go on to tell me how I should implement it. This spelling out in detail how specifically to carry out a project really frustrated me since I knew exactly how to structure and solve problems without precise directions down to the last detail. This is only a sample of my frustration at his involvement in micromanagement of the company. I had long ago gone through the process of managing a company and the last thing I needed was, with due respect, a person with less experience than I not dealing with me on a level of parity and not having respect for my management acumen.

In fact, this meeting proved quite therapeutic, probably for both parties, since it at least cleared the air for better communications. At the meeting he made clear that he required accounting services only, which to this point had been communicated to me in nuance. This disclosure on his part clarified to me once and for all that full management of the company was not in the future. I certainly had enough clues in the past to convey this message, but my assumption, at least in the back of my mind, was that he would at some time in the near future figure out that my management skills were what the company required to forge ahead more efficiently and profitably. In other words, he would become an advocate and invest in my professional growth. This was not a good assumption! I believe, and I can only speak for myself, that many people hold on to situations longer than they should, and only when they are face to face with the reality do they make a decision to change. The actual meeting put an exclamation on the issue and made my future decisions quite clear. The fact was that he needed accounting services and I wanted to keep one foot in the business world, so we agreed to cut my hours in half, which worked for both parties since he would save on consultant fees and I would have my time freed up for new directions I might pursue.

After the meeting, which was quite a catharsis, my stress level went down considerably. Since I no longer was in limbo regarding my career, I would have considerable time on my hands to pursue my writing career, while keeping my business skills still sharply tuned in to real estate and accounting, since these skills certainly apply to my personal assets and who knows when they might be needed as part of my writing career. This was hopefully a win for both sides. As a sidebar, it is indeed curious that for a personality that resists change, when that change is upon me both my interest and creative forces come to the forefront and my "soul" comes alive. These are, in fact, the most interesting times in my life. I believe to this day that if I had been afforded full management of the company, I could have at least doubled the size of the operation, but since my input was only accepted at a lower level of decision-making, the exercise is academic.

Chapter 10

The Sun Comes Shining Through

Now it was time for a new adventure! We were again at that critical juncture, which we have mentioned on more than one occasion, and at this time my energies were at their peak and the upcoming year would indeed be consequential.

As noted earlier, I was constantly updating my financial condition, as I have throughout the years, and verified, for how many times I know not, that I could survive comfortably on unearned income without dipping into any of the principal of our assets. Both of our homes were owned outright and we carried minimal outstanding charges. With these factors verified, we could now begin our new adventure.

The first part of this new adventure was significant indeed in that it involved our primary residence. For almost twenty years, we had lived in a sleepy seaside town south of Boston. This was the dream home to which we had aspired years earlier, and through a diligent plan of saving and investing, we were finally in a position to purchase. As mentioned earlier, the home was purchased in the early 1980s when interest rates on home mortgages were over 16%, if you can believe that. This was one of the challenges we faced at that time, and decided to purchase the home from a developer who was in dire straits to sell this new home because of the high interest rates. We decided to take a gamble, and that again was one of those critical junctures in life when we opted to buy this unfinished home in a slow real estate market. Our belief was that the asset could do nothing but increase in value over the years if we made the challenging decision to purchase the home at this time when the purchase price was quite attractive due to the state of economic affairs in the country, so in we plunged.

The project was quite a challenge since we bought the new home in unfinished condition. In the first two years we added features we thought would certainly increase the value of the home. Additions such as a two-car attached garage, which enlarged the size of the home, and a clay tennis court, with my "sweat equity" as general contractor, saved several thousands of dollars and added quite a touch to the property. Two new decks which, added to the two existing decks, gave us extra space for activities such as cookouts and sunbathing. The dozens of decorative shrubs completed the basics and maximized a real estate asset that would pay off handsomely in the future.

Our almost twenty-year stay in this home in this wonderful little town by the sea south of Boston was almost like being on vacation. We wouldn't trade this period of time in our lives for the world, however, for the last couple of years my wife had been suggesting to me that, although she had been very happy with our existence in our dream home, after twenty years she had thoughts of moving back to the Boston area. The town, probably as close to a postcard as any town in New England, was however, isolated from the activities in the Boston area. Although I resisted her suggestions for a couple of years, my recent second thoughts about my career in the consulting business gave me serious consideration regarding her thoughts concerning a change in lifestyle. We would spend the next several weeks discussing in depth this "revolutionary" concept.

After thoroughly reviewing the financial ramifications of the move, we reviewed the figures until we reached the point where my wife finally told me that she was exhausted and that we must move on to the next phase since she was surely convinced that the financial prognosis was quite positive. Again my compulsion to detail ensured that we had all of our financial bases covered.

We had already decided that we would opt to downsize to a comfortable condominium lifestyle. The logic behind this was that (1) there were only the two of us and we did not need all of the excess space available in our current home, (2) since we had a home in Florida on a golf course, we would choose to spend several weeks a year there, (3) since we love our golf game, we would like to "lock and go," so to speak, and spend several weekends in other New England states and not have to worry about maintaining a home, and (4) since we owned the home outright, we were sitting on quite a large amount of equity.

These concepts did not arise overnight, rather they had been building over the last couple of years and only now did these ideas materialize. They coincided also with my decision to change directions in my consulting business. As mentioned earlier, our creative juices were flowing. We were eager to move on to our next phase, which, hopefully, within a year or less, would move us to another chapter in our lives. The next serious decision that had to be explored was where in the Boston area we would choose to establish residency. This was, of course, quite critical, since we would only liquidate our present home upon locating a residence that would provide for us that quality of life to which we were accustomed.

Exploring the real estate market in the Boston area was an experience that we had not delved into for almost twenty years. The phrase "sticker shock" would be quite appropriate in describing our preliminary exploration.

Our compulsive personalities became quite essential as we began this process. I explained to my wife the seriousness of this process that we were about to begin. Once we put our house on the market for sale, the process would be irreversible and the project must be pursued until we had accomplished that which we started. Therefore, the first step was to verify that the nature and price range of our new condominium would be acceptable before we made this decisive move.

The process would be long and arduous, and there would be many peaks and valleys in the journey. The ability to continue the search, even when we seemed to be at a dead end, was essential. We have discussed on various occasions that resolving those difficult decisions in life requires the ability "not to give up." With this attitude you have already eliminated a large percentage of others who do not have that ability to "stay with the program," regardless of how difficult the journey. This said, we dug in, and began the laborious task of locating that one piece of real estate that would fulfill our rigid requirements. The task would be indeed daunting.

We had a price range in mind and our search began in that price range. For the next month or two, our evenings and weekends were spent reading the real estate section of various newspapers, exploring the internet, visiting with various real estate brokers, and finally going to endless open houses in the greater Boston area.

This is the point in our search at which theory comes face to face with reality. To say that Boston is a "hot" real estate market would be understatement incarnate. We had two specific areas in the greater Boston area that piqued our interest, so we concentrated our efforts in these areas. The first reality that confronted us was the value, or lack thereof, of the properties that we inspected. To stay within our projected price range, the square footage was about 600 square feet! Now that is really small. Secondly, the condition of the large majority of units, given the fact that Boston is an old city, was less than optimal. My intuition told me that the owners of most of these condominiums converted the units from old apartments, threw a coat of paint on the walls, and called them condominiums.

The estimated size requirements for our living space was about double that of those units we inspected. Finally, parking was either non-existent or the space was for rent at prices one might consider exorbitant and were subject to unexpected increases. To add to this less than acceptable situation, in most cases you had to walk a distance to your condominium. To say we were disappointed at this stage of our search would be ironic to say the least. As optimistic as we tend to be, I believe this was the low point of our search. The fact that the Boston area is one of the most attractive in the northeast area of the United States made it a very attractive drawing card and this obviously drew a large and diversified population who sought habitation in the area. This, of course, brought into play the supply and demand equation. The fact that this atmosphere prevailed only further whetted our appetite to live in the area and required that we dig even deeper into our already intensive search. To keep this intensity intact required an almost superhuman effort, which we were prepared to make. Fortunately, our personalities and commitment prepared us for this possible eventuality and kept us looking when things appeared their darkest.

Chapter 11

Off In The Distance, The Dream

Then, out of the clear blue sky, that luck factor popped its head out of this malaise. As I was scanning the local newspaper, I came across an advertisement in the real estate section. There was a large spread for what appeared to be too good to be true, and with our recent experience in search of our ideal living space, I approached the advertisement cautiously. The advertisement boasted of a marina, several restaurants, luxury condominiums, townhouses, and homes on the oceanfront; and the complex was within five to ten minutes from Boston. Could this "dream complex" be anything close to that which it claimed?

My excitement level was again soaring. I could hardly contain my enthusiasm until my wife returned from work and I could break the news. As she entered the house, I flashed the advertisement before her and waited for her response. Living with a person for a number of years, you acquire the ability to anticipate a response to any number of situations. My expectations were rewarded by her enthusiastic response. We were both on such a high, we decided to visit the complex that afternoon, although it would probably be too late to speak to anyone since the representatives would probably have left for the day. Our visit that day would, however, give credence to our initial response to the advertisement or, hopefully not, thrust us back into our, what seemed to be, never-ending search for our home.

It never ceases to amaze me that no matter how may times you go through the process of purchasing real estate, that anticipation creates butterflies in your stomach and each event is as new and refreshing as that first real estate acquisition years ago.

Our approach to the complex was most dynamic with the Boston skyline as a dramatic backdrop less than three miles ahead. The complex itself was on a peninsula jutting out into Boston Harbor. This land, I believe, was wetlands. The developers, however they accomplished the feat, obtained a building permit, and what was most impressive is that they had a "vision" for the entire area.

The first part of our strategy was to take a ride through the complex to experience the ambiance of the overall area. As mentioned, the land was on a peninsula and had a design theme. Along the outer edge by the ocean were a healthy mix of homes, condominiums, stores, restaurants, and the marina. Special consideration was given to coordinate the various attractive structures in such a way that one could appreciate the tasteful design of the maximum open space. There were essentially three views from the peninsula, all of which were magnificent. On one side there was the Boston skyline, which fanned out to the second unobstructed view of the inner islands of Boston Harbor, and finally, to the south, a clear view, over the marshes, of the bay south of Boston.

The specific condominium complex that commanded our interest was the edifice first seen as you approach the peninsula from the south. The actual building is what can only be described as a grand European hotel. The area surrounding the structure was spacious and professionally designed with various types of trees and shrubs. The main entrance approaching the building was a circular driveway that artistically flowed under an overhang, and when followed in one direction led to one of the two entrances to the underground garage. The structure itself was beige textured brick with decorative features over the windows and ornate balconies. The roof was of slate and the edifice gave one the aspect of Victorian luxury in the countryside. So far, two of the elements that were essential in our search were present: (1) the overall area was superb in appearance and was surrounded on three sides by oceanfront, and (2) the structure itself more than fulfilled our earlier expectations and resembled what my wife calls a European luxury hotel. Now we would explore the last element of our requirement for our perfect habitation, that is, the internal makeup of this "grand hotel."

We parked our car in front of the complex where there was a special parking area for visitors. Upon entering the lobby, what was most impressive was the "luxury hotel-like" atmosphere. It began with the oversized chandelier, which attracted your attention upon entering, and as your eyes fell to ground level, the classic stairway to the upper level of the lobby, down the long hallway which led to the outside back landscaped terrace, which was framed by the large double doors.

The lobby itself was done in a laid-back Victorian style and, as I was to have revealed to me later, was used for periodic functions for the owners in the building. What was most impressive was the immaculate condition of the common areas, including the lobby and the outside grounds.

Looking back to that eventful day, I believe both my wife and I were in a state of shock. This marvelous complex was, at risk of sounding trite, like a dream come true and restored our faith in our theory that, if you look long and intensely enough, you will have a great chance of realizing your dreams, and this applies to many other aspects of your life. Upon leaving the area that evening, the only talk we were able to generate on the way home was a discussion of "our" condominium. We had to sleep on pins and needles until our meeting, which we arranged the following morning, with the agent that very day.

That next morning the sunrise was spectacular and we hoped it would be a harbinger for our meeting that day with the real estate agent. We were too excited for breakfast, so a coffee on the road would have to do. Upon approaching the complex, the same enthusiasm was present in our comportment as was present the previous day.

As we entered the lobby there was an office to the right, and we entered and had our first of several meetings with our representative. The office itself was high-tech and had many monitors on one side of the room, which kept an active surveillance of the various common areas of the building. This was a good indication of how the management of the complex approached security of the grounds and reinforced our impressions from our visit the previous day.

The agent, it turned out, was the sister of the building's owner. The building, about eight years old, had been a luxury apartment complex and was being converted to a luxury condominium. This was our first clue that our timing could be indeed fortuitous. More than one unit was available due to the conversion, and we had approached the owner at the beginning of the conversion process, thus making several choice units available. It would also help in the liquidation of our home in terms of timing, since buying and selling homes is contingent, in many cases, upon how quickly you can sell your home, which is tied into when you can buy your new home. The timing is critical to avoid the dreaded "bridge loan," when you must commit to a new mortgage while still paying on your existing mortgage. This can be uncomfortable for some people, even if your home is owned outright, since now you are committing to a new mortgage when your strategy was to use the funds from the sale of your home to pay for the new residence in cash. Being very conservative, I felt an uneasiness committing to a new mortgage, temporary as it may have been, before selling our home and using part of the funds to pay for the new condominium in cash. Since there was more than one condominium available, we assumed the timing would be less of a problem. As it turned out, this was not only not a problem, but also the representative, whom we got to know over the next few weeks, turned out to be very cooperative. We not only had the choice of one of several units, but she would also be open to a contingency offer, that is, the sale would be contingent upon the sale of our home. Later that day, my wife and I agreed that this occasion was meant to be. This is, of course, not scientific, but in life many such occurrences are more fortuitous than scientific.

Before we began our inspection of the various units available, the representative went into detail regarding all of those elements involved in purchasing the condominium, including the price range of the various units. Unbelievably, the unit we would eventually purchase fell within the upper level of our budget! This was the final sign we needed to commit. The package was quite outstanding, including a two-car parking space under the complex which we would own as part of the purchase of the condominium, all new appliances including a washer/dryer in the unit, the unit would be repainted, although upon our inspection it didn't even look as though it needed it, and finally, the condominium which we eventually selected was a large two-bedroom unit with a double French door leading to a spacious balcony overlooking the bay south of Boston. After the inspection, multiple documents were required to be filled out and we had our final meeting with the broker. We would now anxiously wait for the sale of our home.

The ball was again in our court and it was our obligation to ensure that the final outcome was that which we had worked so diligently to accomplish. We had, prior to the beginning of our search for the ideal condominium in the Boston area, done some comparable home sale analyses in our town, and screened several real estate brokerage houses to give our guidelines to the representatives should we decide to sell. All of this homework paid off handsomely when we revisited our broker of choice and gave him the listing. We were unsure as to how long the process would take to sell the home, but we wanted to have the listing in the marketplace as soon as possible, even though we had the back up of our contingency offer on the condominium. Our real estate broker, who was quite aggressive on our behalf in both advertising and holding open houses, added a bit of disruptiveness to our organized system, but the potential reward was certainly worth the inconvenience.

Then one day, less than a month into the listing of the property, our real estate broker informed us that he had an offer on our home. We were, of course, jubilant that he had attracted a buyer so early in the search. Two confluent circumstances occurred which injected that magic into the formula and made the transaction possible. (1) The people who offered to purchase the property lived in the town and knew of the property and wanted to downsize from their larger home to facilitate the expensive college tuition for their daughter. They wanted to stay in the town because of the excellent school system and did not choose to uproot their children. (2) We were at the top of a real estate market wherein homes were turning over almost immediately and had just about reached its peak. Only six months after the sale did we find out that the real estate market was leveling off. The offer we received was more than the listing price. Again, since the transaction was good for both sides, the closing was expedited. Both parties profited from that magical connection when both parties walk away from the closing resulting in a mutually beneficial ending.

The closings, and I use the plural since both the selling of our home and the purchase of our new condominium were accomplished on the same day, were almost anticlimactic since we used so much energy to reach this point. We just about effortlessly completed that boring process which one must endure at closings. The day, however, was quite full, and by the end of the day we were truly exhausted.

Now began the final laborious task of physically moving into our new home. As is the case with all projects which we approach, the details of both liquidating those excessive pieces of furniture, accessories, and other excess baggage were methodically sold, given away, or taken to the transfer station for disposal, and moving those remaining pieces of furniture and accessories to the new home went smoothly. Fortunately for us, our good relationship with the broker at the condominium permitted us to have our hardwood floors, which we decided were essential for our new home, installed prior to the closing. This was a nice concession on her part, but as I mentioned to her, if by some long shot something went wrong at the closing and we could not consummate the purchase, the floors would have been installed and we would be the losers since the installation would have been done at our potential peril. At any rate, the move went very smoothly due to our diligent preplanning. Again our compulsiveness certainly played a key role in the successful conclusion of this major change in our lifestyle. We would now begin the next interesting part of our life.

Chapter 12

What Is A Nickel, And What Is A Dollar?

Entrance into the world of business was accidental in that my training was in political science. This is not a unique revelation since the scenario has probably been played out for many thousands before me and will probably befall as many after me. My goal was to earn a living and that "accident" was simply a pragmatic response to an opportunity that presented itself and since, as mentioned earlier, my childhood lacked an acceptable economic base and resulted in a fixation on things material. The fact that I was absent a father as a role model who could give me that thrust in the right direction was certainly a factor resulting in a circuitous adventure in defining who I was. Mostly missed was that ongoing discussion with a parent who might lead you in the right direction. Again, this has been the lot of many in addition to me. The fact is that my compulsive organization skills and attention to detail fed into the business career into which I fell.

In retrospect, my life was actually out of control, yet organized, if you can follow the logic. I was so focused on building a consulting business, which was not actually leading to that spot I had envisioned, for whatever reason, be it for not having specific benchmarks to which I could hold myself responsible, or whether it was because I did not have that "advocate" to help thrust me in the right direction at the appropriate time, or whether my business plan was unrealistic in terms of a realistic growth curve, was academic. On the one hand I accomplished my financial goals of being able to live on unearned income, but did not realize that material gains in and by themselves are not an end. The control that I must maintain is essential had, in fact, diminished somewhere along the line. More specifically, you can be in control of your material goals and your day-to-day routine that is helping attain those goals, but at the same time the "big picture" of your career escapes you. Loss of one of my main accounts brought this "big picture" into focus. To this point, the cash flow was so rewarding that I hesitated to ask the hard question of whether or not my career was on the right track, not in monetary terms but in terms of responsibility and growth. The cash flow no longer blinded me and forced me to rethink my consulting business on other than a cash flow basis. What I saw was not attractive! I had, for the past several years, been performing essentially accounting obligations and not fulfilling those tasks that I had set for myself years earlier. My goals back then, and they have remained to this day, are to actually manage a company, do growth projections and budgets, and participate at the top level of decision-making in terms of overall corporate policy. I had apparently been lulled to sleep by the monetary rewards and failed to see that the owners for whom I was consulting did not choose to offer me those challenges, or at least share the responsibility of growth and decision-making. Rather, I was used as a very proficient accountant who, since I performed very efficiently at that level, should remain at the level that served their immediate needs, but did not serve mine, and limited my growth into that top management position to which I aspired. I was now to make that fateful decision to either pursue my established goal of looking for that right "advocate" account, which would offer me the opportunity to perform at the level which could truly test my capabilities, or to question continuing in this direction, which might continue to be counterproductive to my goals. Since I had reached "critical mass" economically, should I shift gears and pursue a creative writing career where I was in complete control and simply keep two or three of the main accounts which would consume minimal time and keep my finger in the business pie, so to speak, while allowing me maximum time pursuing my new career in writing? With my lifelong goal of being able to live on unearned income successfully achieved, the choice without hesitation would be to pursue my career as a writer.

Chapter 13

Finally, Convergence Of The Compulsive Personality And The Creative Soul

I now have taken that fateful step which has begun the process of bringing my life into control with a different focus, and truly feel that a large burden has been taken from my shoulders.

It has been a fortuitous convergence of events that has brought me to this new plateau. Interestingly, the initial, and seminal event that sparked this new refocusing of energies was an event generated not from within, but by the unfortunate death of one of my clients. That one event began the redirection of my fixation from business in general and my consulting company, the real goal of which was not being achieved and probably subconsciously I had been denying, to uncovering that creative niche which had laid dormant for these many years. That initial event opened the door for the next, and to this point, unthinkable process of selling our home, which had been an integral part of our lives for almost twenty years.

I had not seriously considered selling our home and moving to Boston, despite the subtle clues being presented to me by my wife, but upon the cutback of one of my main accounts, it now became easier to consider seriously such an option after reviewing the financial situation objectively and looking closely at the large equity position which had been building in our home over the years. It is quite remarkable how your perspective on a situation can radically change when one of the key elements of the equation changes. My focus was no longer on maintaining the status quo revolving around my business and maintaining our current stressful lifestyle, which could have continued until I decided to retire, but as revealed, it would probably have been an unfulfilled journey except for the material aspect of our lives. Rather, change became a new and exciting component in restructuring our lives and priorities. Within this one monumental year we had practically uprooted all that we had constructed in the last twenty years. The financial goals have now been essentially achieved, and you will note that I have laboriously referred to this fact on more than one occasion, which reveals how much of a component this has been in directing my career and over the years has dominated my overall planning. I make no excuses, however, for this fixation due to my less than affluent early childhood experience, but fortunately, with hindsight, recognize this shortcoming in my calculations. I am able finally to see clearly who I can become absent the harness that I had imposed upon myself in "having to make a living."

I presume I could always ask myself what more I could have accomplished in the business world had I that "advocate" or better, had I been my own advocate, as a close friend recently brought to my attention. Valid as this speculation might be, if in fact I had reached that other goal, would I have pursued that dream of becoming a writer? Intriguing as this question may be, I consider myself exceptionally fortunate that the door has been opened, or more precisely, that I have opened the door to this new adventure and the freedom has been given me to explore this, to date, unexplored area of my journey to discover new areas of my persona and hopefully add a deeper meaning as to why we are making this interesting sojourn through life.

I now have the opportunity, at my leisure, to take a more philosophic perspective on where I not only choose to stand, but where I choose to extend myself in terms of self-fulfillment. To this point in my life, my energies had been expended responding to those daily business activities, which in the long term, were not only unproductive in further expanding my universe, rather they were actually counterproductive. My focus was so restricted, I failed to see the larger view of life. I insulated myself from discovering those opportunities that could expand my horizons and permit me the luxury of not only more fully enjoying my leisure time, but to fully utilize that creative energy to generate interesting and insightful statements through my innovative writing. It would have been impossible for me, even a year earlier, to envision sitting in my den overlooking the ocean and manufacturing ongoing new ideas.

Success in life I suggest, to a creative soul, is being in a position where the only restraint on your creative output is yourself. A bonus I didn't even expect is that my obsessive compulsiveness, far from being a burden, is a magic tool that I can utilize to organize my creative writing and keep the projects moving forward on a scheduled basis. Creativity and obsessive behavior seem to be odd bedfellows, but maybe not. In any case, it seems to work for me.

This is not the ending of our journey, but a new beginning.